Developing Numeracy

PRIMARY
MATHS
DICTIONARY

GARDA TURNER

A & C BLACK • LONDON

© Blake Publishing 2003
Additional material © Hilary Koll and Steve Mills 2006

First published in 2003 in Australia by Pascal Press

This edition published in 2006 in the United Kingdom by
A & C Black Publishers Ltd, 38 Soho Square, London W1D 3HB
www.acblack.com

ISBN-10: 0-7136-7850-X
ISBN-13: 978-0-7136-7850-5

A CIP record for this book is available from the British Library.

Written by Garda Turner
Design and layout by The Modern Art Production Group
Publisher: Katy Pike
Series editor: Garda Turner
Editor: Amanda Santamaria

UK consultants: Hilary Koll and Steve Mills

Printed and bound in China through Phoenix Offset

A & C Black uses paper produced with elemental chlorine-free pulp,
harvested from managed sustainable forests.

Introduction

The *Developing Numeracy Primary Maths Dictionary* is an essential guide to the mathematical language and concepts used in primary schools. It has been written with the young reader in mind, giving clear, simple and concise definitions. Most definitions also include a colourful photo or diagram to assist understanding. Worked examples offer further explanation. The words covered come from all strands of the primary mathematics curriculum.

This book is a handy, easy-to-use and easy-to-carry reference for all young pupils. Many everyday words take on a special meaning when we use them in mathematics. This can be confusing for pupils. Understanding mathematical language and symbols is an integral part of learning many mathematical concepts. The dictionary will also aid parents when they are assisting their children at home.

Useful reference charts include mathematical symbols, abbreviations, fraction tables, metric measurement tables, conversion from metric to Imperial measures and Roman numerals.

Contents

abacus
- an instrument made of rods and beads
- used for counting

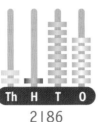

Th H T O

2186

acre
- an Imperial measurement used for measuring the area of large blocks of land

Fields were measured in acres.

acute angle
- an angle that measures between 0° and 90°

add
- to combine things
- join together

addition
- to combine two or more numbers to make one larger number

$$7 + 12 + 9 = 28$$

adjacent
- next to each other

a and b are adjacent angles.

algebra
- a part of mathematics where letters or symbols are used instead of numbers

$$\blacklozenge \div 8 = 64$$

$$42 + \mathbf{y} = 52$$

algorithm
- the formal way of setting out operations to work out the answer

$$\begin{array}{r} 2\ 9\ 4 \\ -\ 1\ 6\ 7 \\ \hline \\ \hline \end{array}$$ This is a subtraction algorithm.

am
- stands for **ante meridiem**
- means the time from midnight to midday (morning)

sunrise

I

analogue clock or watch

– a clock or watch that shows twelve-hour time on a clock face using hands

angle

– an amount of turn measured in degrees (°)

annual

– once every year

anticlockwise

– moving in the opposite direction to the hands on a clock

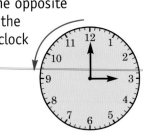

apex

– the vertex that is furthest from the base

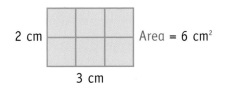

apex

approximation

– very close but not exact

200 is an approximation for 197.

arc

– a part of the circumference of a circle

arc

arc

area

– the size of a surface measured in square units
– the space inside a perimeter

2 cm Area = 6 cm²

3 cm

array

– objects or numbers arranged in rows and columns

ascending order
– in order from smallest to largest

25, 85, 109, 153, 286

These numbers are written
in ascending order.

attribute
– a characteristic of an object
– can be size, colour, thickness,
length etc.

a long, pink, round candy bar

autumn
– the season that follows summer
– September, October, November

average
– is one score that tries to show the
'middle' of a group of scores
– there are three main types of
average: mean, median and mode

axis
– the two scaled straight lines on a
graph are called axes, the x axis
and the y axis

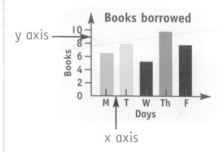

x axis

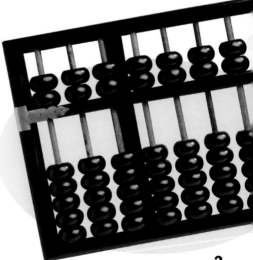

bar graph/chart
– uses bars or columns to show information

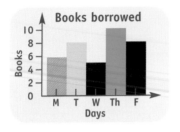

bar line graph
– similar to a bar graph but it uses lines instead of bars to show information

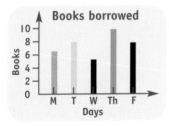

base (number)
– a grouping number
– our number system uses base ten as we group numbers in tens

365

The 6 stands for 6 tens

base (of a shape)
– a line or surface on which something stands

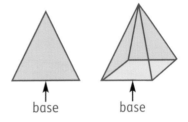

bias
– unfair

A biased die is weighted to make one number come up more often than the others.

billion
– a thousand millions

$1000 \times 1\,000\,000 = 1\,000\,000\,000$

bisect
– to divide something into two equal parts

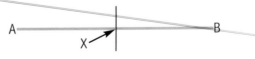

Line AB is bisected at X.
AX is the same length as XB.

block graph
– similar to a bar chart but uses individual blocks joined together to make columns

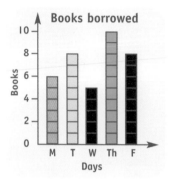

brackets
– symbols used to group things together

$$(9 + 5) \times (7 - 3) = 56$$

Brackets group 9 and 5 together, and 7 and 3 together.

breadth
– another name for width

calculate
– to work something out

9p

27p

18p

Calculate how much money was spent to buy these items.

9p + 27p + 18p = 54p

calculator
– a machine that calculates

calendar
– a time map that tells us what day and month it is

capacity
– the greatest amount something can hold
– is measured in millilitres (ml) and litres (l)

This container has a capacity of 2 litres.

Carroll diagram
– a way of sorting information using rows and columns

	Names that start with S	Names that do not start with S
Names that have 3 letters	Sue Sam	Ben Dan Tom
Names that do not have 3 letters	Suvinder Sally	Luke

Celsius
– a temperature scale that is used to tell how hot or cold something is
– water boils at 100°C and freezes at 0°C

centicube
- a block that is 1 cm wide, 1 cm long and 1 cm deep

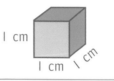

centimetre
- a measurement used for measuring length
- abbreviation is **cm**

centimetres

centre
- the middle
- the midpoint of a circle

centre

century
- 100 years

We are living in the 21st century (from 2000 – 2099).

certain
- things that will definitely happen

chord
- a straight line in a circle that goes from one point on the circumference to another point on the circumference but does not go through the centre

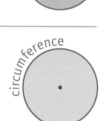
chord

circle
- a 2D shape that has one curved edge only

circumference
- the curved edge of a circle

circumference

classify
- arrange in groups according to attributes

These flowers are classified according to colour.

c

class interval
– the size of groups used when entering data onto a graph

clockwise
– moving in the same direction as the hands on a clock

column
– a vertical arrangement of figures

93
42
7
19

column graph
– a type of bar chart that uses columns to show numbers or amounts of things

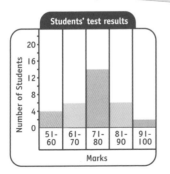

common denominator
– two fractions have a common denominator when they have the same denominator

These fractions have a common denominator of 8:

$\frac{1}{8}$, $\frac{4}{8}$ and $\frac{6}{8}$.

compass
– an instrument that tells us direction

compasses (a pair of)
– an instrument used to draw circles or arcs

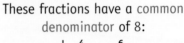

compass points

- the main points are north, south, east, west
- then north-east, south-east, south-west, north-west
- then north-north-east, east-north-east, east-south-east, south-south-east, south-south-west, west-south-west, west-north-west, north-north-west

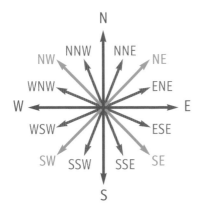

complementary angles

- two angles whose sum is 90°

25° and 65° are complementary angles.

concave

- curved inwards, like a bowl or cave
- a concave 2D shape has one or more vertices that point inwards

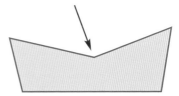

concentric circles

- two or more circles which have the same centre

cone

- a 3D object that has a circular base and one vertex

congruent

- having exactly the same size and shape

These balls are congruent.

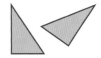

These triangles are congruent.

consecutive numbers
– numbers which follow one another

17, 18, 19, 20
are consecutive numbers.

conversion graph
– allows us to change one unit of something to another, like pounds to Euros

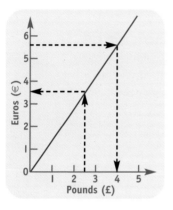

convert
– change

The fraction $\frac{1}{2}$ can be converted to a decimal (0·5) or a percentage (50%).

convex
– curved outwards
– a convex 2D shape has all its vertices pointing outwards

coordinates
– two numbers (or letters) which tell a position on a grid
– the horizontal number is written before the vertical number
– they are written in brackets with a comma between

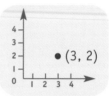

(3, 2) are the coordinates for the point on the chart.

cross-section
– what you see when an object is cut through

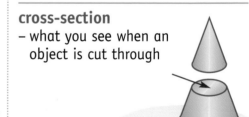

cube (a number)
– to multiply three lots of the same number together

three cubed (3^3)
3 x 3 x 3 = 27

ten cubed (10^3)
10 x 10 x 10 = 1000

cube (shape)
– a 3D object which has six identical square faces

cubic number
– a number formed when three lots of another number are multiplied together

$$7 \times 7 \times 7 = 343 \quad (7^3 = 343)$$

343 is a cubic number.

cubic measure
– is used to measure volume

– measurements include cubic centimetre (cm^3) and cubic metre (m^3)

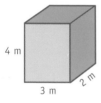

4 m

3 m

2 m

The volume of this box is 24 m^3.

cuboid
– a rectangular prism, like a cereal box

cylinder
– a 3D object that has two circular ends and a curved surface joining the ends

data

– a collection of information such as facts or measurements

What are the most popular fruits eaten by your friends?

This is the data.

Fruit	Number of people
orange	3
apple	4
plum	6
peach	10
grape	9
watermelon	12

date

– tells us what day, month and year it is

27th April 2007
(short date 27/4/07)

day

– twenty-four hours which start and end at midnight

deca

– a prefix meaning ten

decagon – a 10-sided figure
decade – 10 years

decade

– 10 years

2000, 2001, 2002, 2003, 2004, 2005, 2006, 2007, 2008, 2009 make a decade.

decagon

– a polygon with ten straight sides

decimal

– a number that lies between two whole numbers, that is written with a decimal point

decimal point

– the dot that separates the 'whole number' digits from the 'part number' digits of a decimal

4·6 means there are 4 whole ones and 6 tenths.

decimal place

– the number of digits to the right of a decimal point

4·67 has 2 decimal places and 63·284 has 3 decimal places.

decrease

– to make smaller

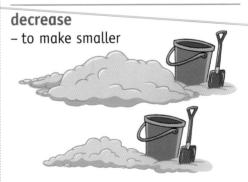

The sand pile has decreased in size.

deduct
– to take away from

> Deduct £4 from your pay.
> (Take £4 away from your pay.)

degree
– a measurement used to measure angles
– also a measurement used to measure temperature
– uses the symbol °

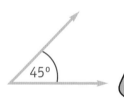

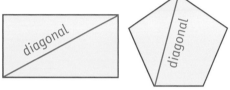

26°

45°

denominator
– the bottom number in a fraction

$\frac{1}{4}$ 4 is the denominator.

descending order
– in order from largest to smallest

> 204, 189, 132, 87, 31, 13
> These numbers are written in descending order.

diagonal
– a straight line that is drawn inside a shape from one vertex to another
– a straight line that is not horizontal or vertical

diagonal

diagonal

diagram
– a picture used to describe something

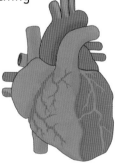

a diagram of a heart

diameter
– a straight line drawn from one point on the circumference of a circle through the centre to another point on the circumference of the circle

diameter

13

die (plural is dice)
– a numbered cube that is used in games

difference
– the amount by which one number is bigger or smaller than another number

> The difference between 7 and 11 is 4.

digit
– one of our numerals

> 0, 1, 2, 3, 4, 5, 6, 7, 8, 9 are the digits we use.

digital clock (or watch)
– a clock or watch that has no hands
– they use numerals to show the time

digital clock

digital watch

dimension
– a measure of size
– shapes with two dimensions are known as 2D shapes
– shapes with three dimensions are known as 3D shapes

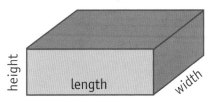

height

length

width

Length, height and width are dimensions. This shape is 3D.

discount
– a reduction in money

£25 £23

The discount is £2.

distance
– the length between two points

The distance between the children is 2 metres.

2 m

divide

– to share something into groups

These 12 feathers are divided
into 3 groups.

division

– the act of dividing into groups

$$6\overline{)72} \quad 12$$

divisor

– the number used to divide by

$$36 \div 9 = 4$$

9 is the divisor.

dodecagon

– a polygon with
12 straight sides

dodecahedron

– a 3D shape with
12 straight sides
– a polygon with
12 faces

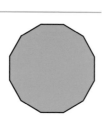

dominoes

– rectangular tiles with one face
divided into two parts marked
with dots
– used to play games

dotty paper

– paper marked with a regular dot
pattern
– can be square or isometric

square dots   isometric dots

double

– make twice as many or twice
as big

Double 6 is 12.
Double 3 kg is 6 kg.

dozen

– 12 things together

15

edge
– where two faces meet

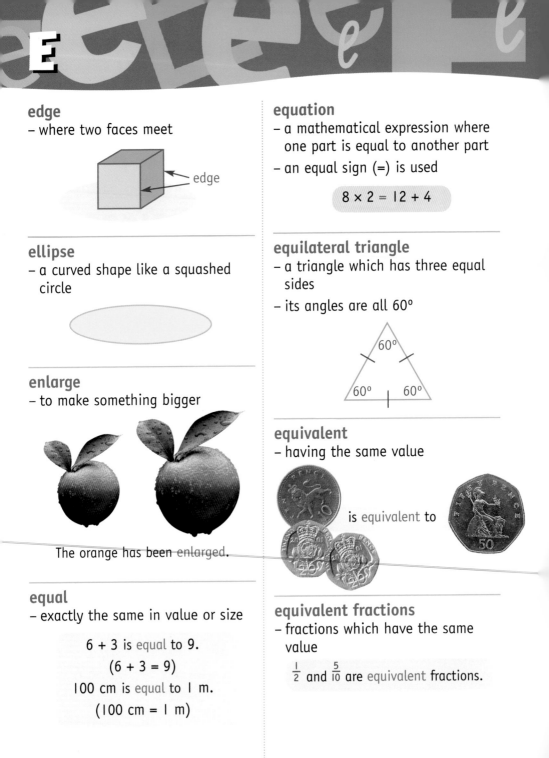

ellipse
– a curved shape like a squashed circle

enlarge
– to make something bigger

The orange has been enlarged.

equal
– exactly the same in value or size

6 + 3 is equal to 9.
(6 + 3 = 9)
100 cm is equal to 1 m.
(100 cm = 1 m)

equation
– a mathematical expression where one part is equal to another part
– an equal sign (=) is used

$$8 \times 2 = 12 + 4$$

equilateral triangle
– a triangle which has three equal sides
– its angles are all 60°

equivalent
– having the same value

is equivalent to

equivalent fractions
– fractions which have the same value

$\frac{1}{2}$ and $\frac{5}{10}$ are equivalent fractions.

estimate
– to make a close guess
– it is never an exact answer

> 215 + 683
> 900 is the estimation.

evaluate
– to work out the value

> $\bigodot - 5 = 9$ Evaluate for $\bigodot$.
> $\bigodot = 14$

even number
– a whole number that can be divided exactly by 2
– ends in 0, 2, 4, 6 or 8

> 112 is an even number.
> 221 is not an even number.

exchange
– swap

H	T	U
6	³⁄4̶	¹2
- 2	1	5
4	2	7

Here one ten is exchanged for ten ones.

face
– a surface of a solid object

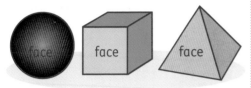

---

factor
– a whole number that divides exactly into another number

12 ÷ 4 = 3 so 4 is a factor of 12.
Other factors of 12 are
1, 2, 3, 6, 12.

Fibonacci sequence
– a sequence of numbers where each term, after the second term, is made by adding the previous two terms

1, 1, 2 (1 + 1), 3 (2 + 1),
5 (3 + 2), 8 (5 + 3) etc.
1, 1, 2, 3, 5, 8, 13, 21, 34, 55 ...

---

first
– comes before anything else

formula
– a rule
– shows how to work something out

The formula for finding the area of a rectangle is A = l × b.

A stands for area, l for length and b for breadth.

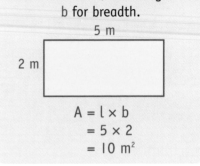

$$A = l \times b$$
$$= 5 \times 2$$
$$= 10 \text{ m}^2$$

---

fortnight
– 2 whole weeks
– 14 days

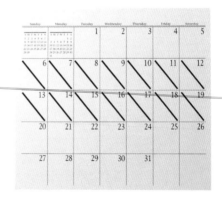

fraction

– a part of a number group or object split into equal parts

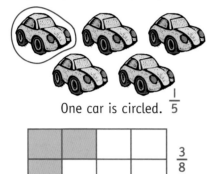

One car is circled. $\frac{1}{5}$

$\frac{3}{8}$

frequency

– how often something happens

I	5	3	2
5	2	3	3
2	3	6	I
3	I	4	3

In this table:

 3 has a frequency of 6.

4 has a frequency of I.

frequency table

– a way of recording the number of times something happens or how many of certain things we have

Type of vehicle	Frequency
Bus	6
Bicycle	4
Lorry	I
Car	5
Van	2

geoboard
- a studded base board
- rubber bands are stretched around the studs to make shapes

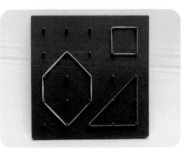

geometry
- a part of mathematics which deals with 2D and 3D space
- shapes, objects, size, position

googol
- is the number written as 1 followed by 100 zeros

$$10^{100}$$

gram
- a measurement used for mass
- 1000 grams = 1 kilogram
- abbreviation is **g**

These strawberries weigh 250 g.

graph
- a diagram that shows a collection of data

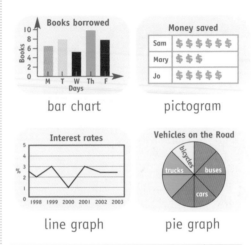

bar chart   pictogram

line graph   pie graph

greater than
- a symbol can be used to say greater than (>)

7 > 2 tells us that 7 is greater than 2.

grouping
- sharing objects into groups that are equal in size

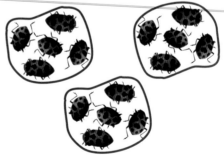

15 beetles are shared into 3 groups.

handspan
– the distance between the tips of the thumb and little finger on an outstretched hand

hectare
– a measurement used to record large areas
– the abbreviation is **ha**

Fields are measured in hectares.

height
– the vertical distance from top to bottom

The height of this model house is 3.9 cm.

3.9 cm

hemisphere
– half a sphere
– Earth is divided into the Northern Hemisphere and the Southern Hemisphere

heptagon
– a polygon that has 7 straight sides

hexagon
– a polygon that has 6 straight sides

Hindu-Arabic number system
– our number system
– was developed from the Hindus and Arabs
– uses numerals that include zero as a place keeper

0, 1, 2, 3, 4, 5, 6, 7, 8, 9

21

horizontal
- parallel to the horizon
- side to side

← horizon

This photo shows the horizon.

hour
- 60 minutes

The amount of time between 1 o'clock
and 2 o'clock is one hour.

hundredth
- one part out of 100 equal parts

hypotenuse
- the side opposite the right angle
  in a right-angled triangle

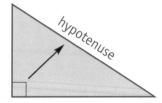

hypotenuse

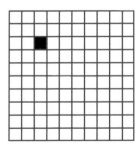

icosahedron
– a 3D shape with 20 faces

Imperial units
– the units of measurement used as part of an old measuring system that are different from metric units

Imperial units include inches, feet, yards, miles, ounces, pounds, stones, pints and gallons.

impossible
– events that will definitely not happen

improper fraction
– a fraction which has a numerator bigger than its denominator

$\frac{3}{2}$ and $\frac{10}{7}$ are improper fractions.

increase
– to make something larger

The amount of water in the bowl will increase.

infinite (adjective)
– never ending
– has no boundaries

The set of even numbers is an infinite set. There is no last number.

infinity (noun)
– the state of being endless
– cannot be given an exact value
– uses the symbol ∞

integer
– is a whole number

7 is an integer.
315 is an integer.
-12 is an integer.

intersect
– to cut across each other

This sign is used when roads intersect.

These are intersecting lines.

intersection
– where two things cross and overlap

The intersection on this Venn diagram is shaded in red.

inverse
– in reverse

> The inverse of multiplying by 7 is dividing by 7.
>
> The inverse of adding 11 is subtracting 11.

irregular polygon
– a shape with sides that are not equal in length or angles that are not equal in size

an irregular pentagon

isometric dotty paper

isosceles triangle
– has two equal sides
– the angles opposite the equal sides are also equal

K

key
– the information needed to read a picture graph or diagram

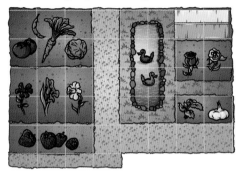

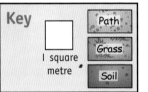

kilo
– a prefix meaning one thousand

> kilogram – 1000 grams
> kilometre – 1000 metres

kilogram
– a measure of mass
– abbreviation is **kg**

This dog weighs 7 kg.

kilometre
– a measure for long distances
– abbreviation is **km**
– 1 km = 1000 m

The length of a road is measured in kilometres.

kite
– a 4-sided 2D shape
– has two pairs of equal adjacent sides

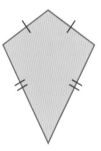

leap year
– has 366 days

– in a leap year February has 29 days

– happens every 4th year

2024 is a leap year.
2028 is the next leap year.

February						
Sun	Mon	Tues	Wed	Thur	Fri	Sat
	1	2	3	4	5	6
7	8	9	10	11	12	13
14	15	16	17	18	19	20
21	22	23	24	25	26	27
28	29					

This calendar shows February
in a leap year.

least
– the smallest amount

The small bottle
holds the least oil.

length
– the distance from
end to end

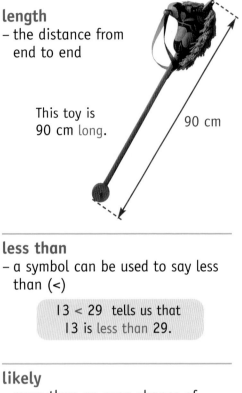

This toy is
90 cm long.

90 cm

less than
– a symbol can be used to say less
than (<)

13 < 29 tells us that
13 is less than 29.

likely
– more than an even chance of
happening but not certain

line graph
– uses axes and lines to show data

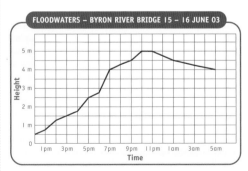

FLOODWATERS – BYRON RIVER BRIDGE 15 – 16 JUNE 03

lines

– parallel lines are straight lines that never meet no matter how far they are drawn

– perpendicular lines meet at right angles

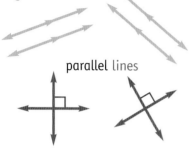

parallel lines

perpendicular lines

line symmetry

– a shape has line symmetry if both halves match exactly when it is folded on the line of symmetry

– line of symmetry is also called the axis of symmetry

line of
symmetry

litre

– a measure used for liquids

– abbreviation is l

This bottle can measure 4 l.

lowest common denominator

– the lowest number that can be used for the denominator of a group of fractions

$$\frac{1}{2}, \frac{2}{3}, \frac{1}{6}, \frac{3}{4}$$

The lowest common denominator for this group is 12.

$$\frac{6}{12}, \frac{8}{12}, \frac{2}{12}, \frac{9}{12}$$

magic square
- a square filled with numbers
- the numbers in each row, each column, each diagonal all have the same sum

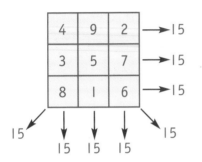

Each row, column and diagonal totals 15.

map
- a diagram of a country or place that shows its position in the world
- always drawn to scale

mass
- matter in an object
- is measured in grams, kilograms, tonnes

The mass of the fruit is 1 kg 385 g.

maximum
- the most

The maximum speed allowed is 60 miles per hour.

mean
- a type of average

8, 19, 7, 9, 7

To find the mean add all the scores and divide by how many scores there are.

8 + 19 + 7 + 9 + 7 = 50

50 ÷ 5 = 10   mean = 10

measure
- to work out the size or amount of an object or distance

median
- the middle score (or scores) when a set of scores are written in order of size

Scores: 3, 3, 5, ⑦, 10, 10, 12
Median: 7

- if there is no middle score, the median is halfway between the two middle scores

Scores: 3, ④, ⑥ 9
Median: 5

metre
- a measure used for length or distance
- abbreviation is **m**

Running races are measured in metres.

metric units
- the units of measurement used as part of our decimal system

Metric units include millimetres, centimetres, metres, kilometres, grams, kilograms, millilitres and litres.

milometer
- an instrument that measures distance travelled in miles

millennium
- a thousand years

All the years from 2000 to 2999 make a millennium.

milli
- a prefix meaning one-thousandth

millimetre – one-thousandth of 1 metre
millilitre – one-thousandth of 1 litre

millilitre
- a measure used for small amounts of liquid
- abbreviation is **ml**

30 ml
20 ml
10 ml
5 ml

Medicines are measured in millilitres.

millimetre
– a measure used for small lengths
– abbreviation is **mm**

15 mm

This eraser is 15 millimetres wide.

million
– a thousand thousands

1 000 000

minimum
– the least amount

The minimum temperature for the last 24 hours was 0°C.

minus
– another word for subtract or take away

24 minus 7 is 17.

24 – 7 = 17

– the word we sometimes use to describe a negative number such as temperature

It is minus six degrees.

minute
– a measure of time
– 60 seconds is one minute

minute hand
– the large hand on a clock that tells the minutes
– it moves once around the clock face every hour

minute hand

mirror image
– an image which reflects another image exactly

mixed number
– has a whole number and a proper fraction

$6\frac{1}{2}$ is a mixed number.

whole number   proper fraction

mode
– is the score that occurs most often in a set of scores

> Scores: 4, 5, 7, 7, 8, 4, 7, 6, 5
> Mode: 7

model
– a small copy that shows what something looks like

a model train engine

month
– a measure of time
– 28, 29, 30 or 31 days
– there are 12 months in a year

> 30 days has September,
> April, June and November.
> All the rest have 31
> Except February alone,
> Which has 28 days clear
> And 29 days each leap year.

multiple
– a number that can be exactly divided by another

> 49 ÷ 7 = 7
> 49 is a multiple of 7 as it can be exactly divided by 7.

multiplicand
– the number being multiplied by another

> 6 × 9 = 54
> 6 is the multiplicand.

multiplication
– a quick way of repeatedly adding the same number to find a total

> 4 + 4 + 4 + 4 + 4
> is the same as 5 x 4.

multiplier
– the number that is doing the multiplying

> 6 × 9 = 54
> 9 is the multiplier.

negative number
– a number less than zero
– written with a minus sign (–3 is negative three)

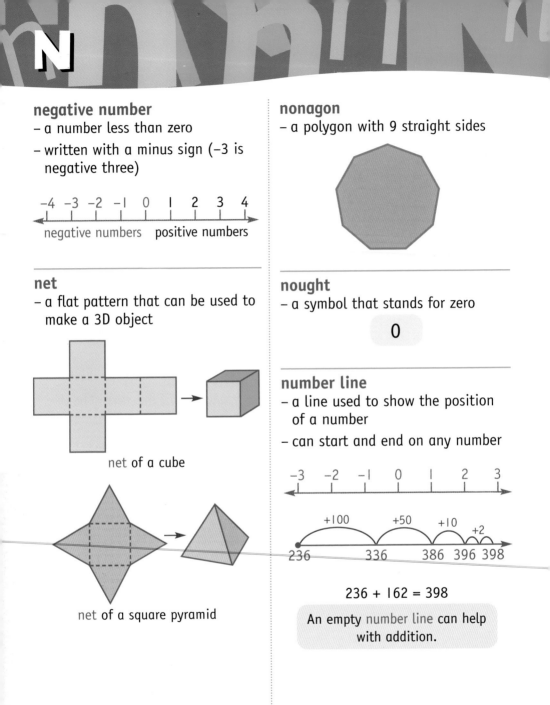

$$-4 \quad -3 \quad -2 \quad -1 \quad 0 \quad 1 \quad 2 \quad 3 \quad 4$$

negative numbers   positive numbers

net
– a flat pattern that can be used to make a 3D object

net of a cube

net of a square pyramid

nonagon
– a polygon with 9 straight sides

nought
– a symbol that stands for zero

0

number line
– a line used to show the position of a number
– can start and end on any number

$$-3 \quad -2 \quad -1 \quad 0 \quad 1 \quad 2 \quad 3$$

+100   +50   +10   +2

236   336   386   396   398

236 + 162 = 398

An empty number line can help with addition.

number sentence
- a sentence written using numerals and signs
- shows a relationship between numbers

$$(7 - 4) \times 8 = 24$$
is a number sentence.

numeral
- a symbol (or group of symbols) that stands for a number

0, 1, 2, 3, 4, 5, 6, 7, 8, 9
are the numerals we use in the metric system.

numerator
- the top number in a fraction
- tells us how many parts we have

$\frac{5}{8}$ 5 is the numerator.

It tells us that we have 5 eighths.

oblong
– another name for a rectangle that is not a square

obtuse angle
– is an angle larger than a right angle but smaller than a straight angle
– measures between 90° and 180°

octagon
– a polygon that has eight straight sides

octahedron
– a 3D shape with 8 faces

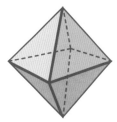

odd number
– a number that cannot be divided exactly by two
– ends in 1, 3, 5, 7 or 9

15, 69, 441
are all odd numbers.

operation
– a process of doing something to numbers or shapes

These are the four main number operations:
addition 5 + 7 + 9
subtraction 259 – 165
multiplication 28 × 36
division 267 ÷ 13

ordering
– placing a group in order according to a given instruction, eg size, weight, length etc

These children are ordered according to height.

8, 23, 41, 88, 107
These numbers are in ascending order.

order of operations
- work everything inside brackets first
- then work all the × and ÷ from left to right
- lastly work all the + and − from left to right

$$7 \times (8 + 3) - 35 \div 7 = 7 \times 11 - 35 \div 7$$
$$= 77 - 5$$
$$= 72$$

order of rotational symmetry
- the number of times a shape will fit into its outline when rotated through one full turn

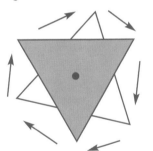

This triangle has an order of rotational symmetry of 3.

ordinal number
- tells position
- 1st, 2nd, 3rd, 4th, 5th etc.

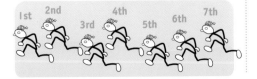

origin
- the point (0,0) where the axes of a graph meet

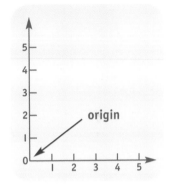

oval
- a closed curve that looks like a squashed circle

These sweets have an oval shape.

P

pair
- two together
- to make twos

a pair of shoes

palindrome
- reads the same backwards and forwards

676   1380831

palindromic numbers

parallel lines
- lines which stay the same distance apart along their whole length
- they can be curved or straight
- they do not need to be the same length as each other

parallel lines

parallelogram
- a special quadrilateral
- opposite sides are parallel
- opposite angles are equal

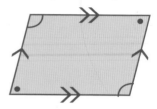

partition
- to split a number into parts to show the value of each digit

27 961 =
20 000 + 7000 + 600 + 90 + 1

pattern
- numbers or objects that are arranged following a rule

1, 6, 11, 16, 21, 26
The rule is to add 5.

Train tracks are parallel.

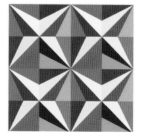

This pattern is made using triangles.

pentagon
– a polygon that has 5 straight sides

percent (%)
– out of 100

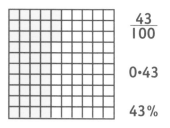

$$\frac{43}{100}$$

$$0\cdot43$$

$$43\%$$

perimeter
– the distance around the outside of a shape
– add the lengths of all the sides

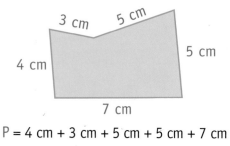

P = 4 cm + 3 cm + 5 cm + 5 cm + 7 cm

P = 24 cm

perpendicular lines
– lines that intersect at right angles

perpendicular lines

The pole and cross bar are perpendicular to each other.

perspective
– the appearance of objects affected by size and position

This photograph of street lights shows perspective.

pi (π)
– the ratio of the circumference of a circle to its diameter
– is equal to $\frac{22}{7}$
– does not have an exact decimal value ($\approx 3 \cdot 14$)

Circumference = π × diameter
$\qquad$ = π × 10
$\qquad$ = 31·4 cm

pictogram
– uses pictures to represent data
– a key is used to interpret the pictures

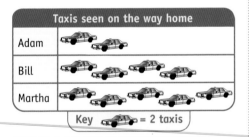

Taxis seen on the way home	
Adam	
Bill	
Martha	

Key = 2 taxis

pie graph/chart
– drawn in a circle
– sectors are used to represent data

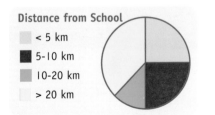

Distance from School
- < 5 km
- 5-10 km
- 10-20 km
- > 20 km

place value
– value according to place in a number

THTU
7382

The place value of the 3 is hundreds because it is in the hundreds place.
The value of the 3 is 300.

plan
– a diagram that shows a view of the whole structure

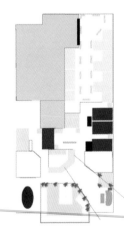

a floor plan of a house

plane shape
– a 2D shape that is drawn on a flat surface

These are plane shapes.

P

plus

– another word for add

50 pence plus 20 pence equals 70 pence.

pm

– stands for **p**ost **m**eridiem

– means the time from midday to midnight (afternoon and evening)

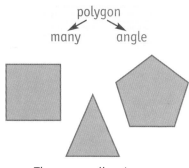

polygon

– a 2D shape with three or more sides and angles

– name comes from Greek words meaning many and angle

These are all polygons.

polyhedron

– a 3D object that has polygons as faces

– a regular polyhedron has all congruent faces

– pyramids and prisms are polyhedrons

polyomino

– a shape made from squares which are all the same size

Some polyominos are:

domino (2 squares)

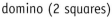

triomino (3 squares)

tetromino (4 squares)

pentomino (5 squares)

39

P

positive number

– a number larger than zero

6, 24½ and 0·57 are all positive numbers.

power of

– the power of a number is shown by an index number
– to find a power, a number is multiplied by itself a number of times

8^3 is 8 to the power of three.
($8 \times 8 \times 8$)

2^7 is 2 to the power of seven.
($2 \times 2 \times 2 \times 2 \times 2 \times 2 \times 2$)

prime factor

– a factor that is a prime number

The prime factors of 12 are $2 \times 2 \times 3$.

prime number

– a number that has only two factors: itself and one

13 is a prime number.
Its only factors are 1 and 13.

prism

– a type of 3D shape that has two identical end faces whose shape give the prism its name
– all other faces are rectangles

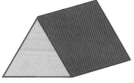

a triangular prism

probability

– the chances of something happening
– words such as *possible*, *certain*, *unlikely*, *sure*, *impossible*, *most likely* etc. are used for probability
– probabilities are often described using fractions, decimals or percentages

It is likely to rain tomorrow.
It is certain to rain this year.

The probability of rolling a 4 on a die is ⅙ .

probability scale
– probabilities can be marked on a scale from 0 (impossible) to 1 (certain)

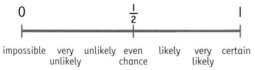

product
– the answer when two or more numbers are multiplied

$$7 \times 3 = 21$$
21 is the product.

$$15 \times 3 \times 7 = 315$$
315 is the product.

proper fraction
– the numerator is smaller than the denominator

$$\frac{1}{3}, \ \frac{2}{5}, \ \frac{8}{10}, \ \frac{21}{37}$$
are all proper fractions.

proportion
– an amount of a whole number or group, described as a fraction, decimal or percentage

The proportion of animals that are cats is $\frac{1}{4}$.

protractor
– an instrument used to measure or draw angles

pyramid
– a 3D object
– it has one base which gives the pyramid its name
– all other faces are triangles

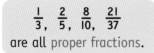

quadrant
– one part of an area that has been divided into four equal parts

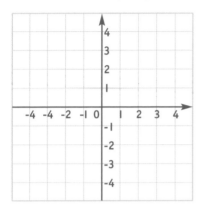

There are four quadrants on this graph.

– a quarter of a circle, formed by two radii drawn at right angles to each other

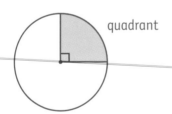

quadrant

quadrilateral
– a polygon with four straight sides

quarter
– one of four equal parts of a group or object
– written as $\frac{1}{4}$

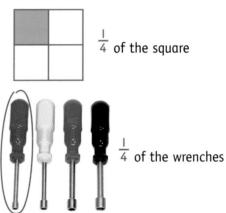

$\frac{1}{4}$ of the square

$\frac{1}{4}$ of the wrenches

quotient
– the answer when one number is divided by another

$$36 \div 9 = 4$$
4 is the quotient

radius
– the distance from the centre of a circle to the circumference

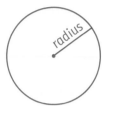

random
– without any pattern or plan

choosing at random

range
– the difference between the lowest and highest scores in a group of scores

3, 6, 9, 1, 9, 4, 3, 5, 7
The range of this group of scores is (9 – 1) 8.

ratio (:)
– compares two or more like quantities

The ratio of cats to dogs is 1:3.

rectangle
– a special quadrilateral
– all angles are right angles
– opposite sides are equal

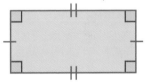

recurring decimal
– some numbers in the decimal keep repeating
– the repeating numbers have repeating dots over them
– a never-ending decimal

$$\frac{1}{3} \; (1 \div 3) = 0{\cdot}33333333333333 \text{ etc.}$$
$$= 0{\cdot}\dot{3}$$
$$\frac{3}{11} \; (3 \div 11) = 0{\cdot}2727272727 \text{ etc.}$$
$$= 0{\cdot}\dot{2}\dot{7}$$

R

reduce
– to make smaller

REDUCE SPEED

Slow down! The speed must become smaller.

reflect
– to show the reflection of a shape on the other side of a mirror line

mirror lines

reflection
– a shape or object as seen in a mirror

reflective symmetry
– another name for line symmetry

reflex angle
– an angle that measures between 180° and 360°

regular polygon
– a polygon that has all sides equal
– it also has all angles equal

This is a regular hexagon.

remainder
– the amount left over when one number cannot be divided exactly by another

17 ÷ 7 = 2 with 3 left over

3 is the remainder.

revolution
– an angle that measures 360°
– a complete turn through 4 right angles

R

rhombus
– a special quadrilateral
– all sides are equal
– opposite sides are parallel
– opposite angles are equal

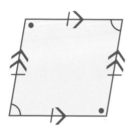

right angle
– an angle that measures 90°

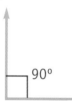

right-angled triangle
– a triangle that has one right angle

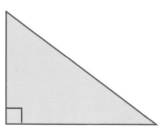

Roman numerals
– a number system used by the ancient Romans
– I, V, X, L, C, D, M are the symbols used

MDCLXX = 1670

This clock has Roman numerals.

rotation
– to turn a shape about a point called the centre of rotation

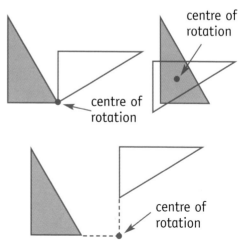

centre of rotation
centre of rotation
centre of rotation

R

rotational symmetry

– when a shape looks the same in different positions as it is turned at a fixed point, it has rotational symmetry

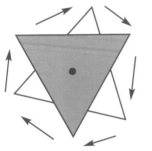

rounding

– giving an approximate number

– we can round to the nearest whole number, multiple of ten, hundred or thousand and so on, or even to the nearest tenth or hundredth

– find which multiple the number is closest to

> 4539 is closer to 4500 than 4600 when rounding to the nearest hundred.
>
> 7764 is closer to 8000 than 7000 when rounding to the nearest thousand.

row

– numbers or objects in a horizontal line

2, 4, 6, 8, 10, 12

A row of even numbers.

A row of paper people.

rule

– an instruction that applies to a sequence of numbers or a pattern

> 1, 2, 4, 8, 16
> Rule: double to get the new term.

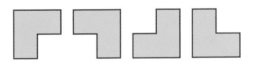

> Rule: turn shape 90° clockwise.

scale
– the ratio of the length shown to the real length it represents

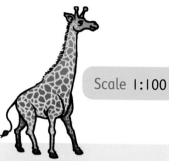

Scale 1:100

The picture is 4 cm high so the giraffe is really 400 cm high.

scale drawing
– enlarging or decreasing the size of a drawing to a given scale

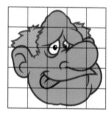

scalene triangle
– a triangle that has sides of different lengths
– the angles are different sizes

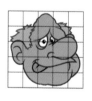

4 cm   2 cm

5 cm

scales
– instruments used to weigh objects
– also used to compare masses

season
– there are 4 seasons in a year: Spring, Summer, Autumn, Winter
– each season is 3 months long

Spring: March, April, May (92 days)

Summer: June, July, August (92 days)

Autumn: September, October, November
(91 days)

Winter: December, January, February
(90 or 91 days)

second
– a very short measure of time
– there are 60 seconds in 1 minute

section
– a part of a whole

These are sections of mandarin.

sector
– a part of a circle bounded by two
  radii and an arc

segment
– a part of a circle bounded by a
  chord and an arc

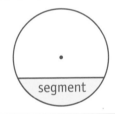

semicircle
– half a circle

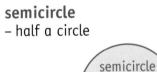

sequence
– a list of numbers or objects which
  are in a special order

> 1, 1, 2, 3, 5, 8, 13 ...
> This is a special sequence called
> the Fibonacci sequence.

set

- a collection of objects or numbers
- each member is called an element of the set

Spring, Summer, Autumn, Winter
This is the set of seasons in a year.

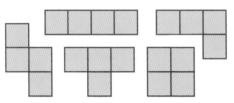

This is a set of tetrominos.

set square

- an instrument shaped like a right-angled triangle
- it can be used to draw right angles
- it can also be used to draw parallel lines

sharing

- putting into equal groups or parts

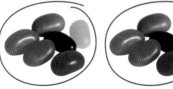

These 12 sweets are shared into two equal groups.

side

- one of the lines that form a 2D shape

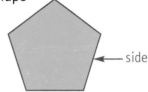

A pentagon has 5 straight sides.

side view

- what you see when you look at an object from the side

sign

- a symbol used instead of words

+, %, >, π, √, ≈

These are some signs we use in maths.

size

- how big an object is

A lion is a large cat.

S

slide
– another word for translation

solid
– an object that has three dimensions: length, height and width

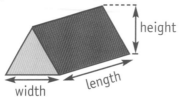

sort
– to place things into like groups

These are sorted into fruits and vegetables.

fruits

vegetables

speed
– how fast something is moving

This rollercoaster is travelling at 75 kilometres per hour (75 km/h).

sphere
– a 3D object shaped like a ball

spinner
– a disc that can be spun to show numbers or colours at random
– it is used in games of chance

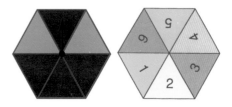

spiral
- an open curve that winds around
- can be endless

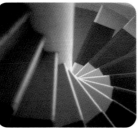

spring
- the season that follows winter
- March, April, May

square (a number)
- to multiply a number by itself

three squared (3^2)

$3 \times 3 = 9$

ten squared (10^2)

$10 \times 10 = 100$

square (shape)
- a polygon with four equal sides and four right angles

square measure
- is the measurement used when finding area

The area of a tennis court is measured in square metres (m^2).

square number
- when a whole number is multiplied by itself the answer is a square number
- a square number can always form a square pattern

$7 \times 7 = 49$

49 is a square number.

$7 \times 7 =$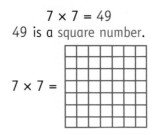

square root (√)

– of a given number is the number that when multiplied by itself, makes the given number

$$\sqrt{81} = 9 \text{ because } 9 \times 9 = 81$$

straight angle

– an angle which looks like a straight line

– always measures 180° (2 right angles)

straight line

– the shortest distance between two points

The shortest distance between Smelly Swamp and Golden Sands is the line AB.

strategy

– a method for working something out

$$73 \times 4$$

A good strategy for multiplying by 4 is to double and double again.

73 doubled = 146 and
146 doubled = 292
so 73 × 4 = 292

statistics

– facts and figures presented in numbers

– information is collected by survey

subtract

– to take one number away from another, or find the difference between two numbers

$$12 - 7 = 5$$

sum

– the total when numbers are added

$$3 + 5 + 9 = 17$$

17 is the sum of 3, 5 and 9.

S

summer
– the season that follows spring
– June, July, August

supplementary angles
– two angles that total 180°
– together they make a straight angle

120° 60°

60° and 120° are
supplementary angles.

77° 103°

103° and 77° are
supplementary angles.

surface
– the top or outside layer of an object
– it can be flat or curved

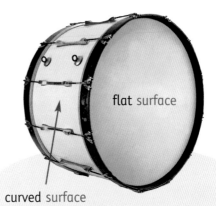

flat surface

curved surface

surface area
– the total area of all the surfaces of a 3D object

The surface area of this square pyramid is the area of the square base plus the areas of the four triangular sides.

survey
– to collect facts or data about a topic

Sport	Tally	Total
Tennis	╫╫ ╫╫ ╫╫ ╫╫ ||	22
Cricket	╫╫ ╫╫ ╫╫	15
Basketball	╫╫ ╫╫ ╫╫ |||	18
Rugby	╫╫ ╫╫ ╫╫ ╫╫ |||\	24
Golf	╫╫ ╫╫ ╫╫ ╫╫		21

100 people were surveyed about their favourite sport.

symbol
– a sign or letter used instead of words

+ (plus), π (pi), √ (square root), ≠ (is not equal to)

symmetry
– there are two main types of symmetry: line (or reflective) symmetry and rotational symmetry

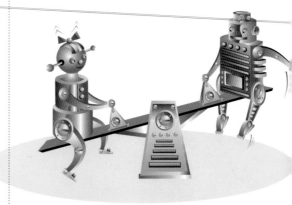

table
– numbers or quantities arranged in rows and columns

SNACK AROUND THE WORLD

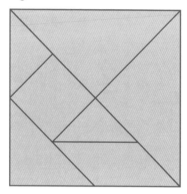

	Hotdog	Coffee	Hamburger
New York	$2.50	$1.75	$3.10
Hong Kong	$4.25	$3.95	$6.40
Vancouver	$3.35	$2.85	$4.50
London	£3.00	£4.00	£5.10
Singapore	$3.35	$1.95	$3.90

tables
– a short name for all the multiplication facts

take away
– to find the difference between two things or numbers
– to subtract

17 take away 9
$$17 - 9 = 8$$

tally marks
– marks used to help when counting a large number
– they are drawn in bundles of five

卌 卌 卌 卌 卌 ||| = 28

tangram
– a traditional Chinese puzzle
– a square cut into one parallelogram, one square and five triangles

temperature
– how hot or cold a thing is

The temperature is hot.

The temperature is cold.

T

term
– one of the parts (elements) of a sequence

> 4, 8, 12, 16, 20
>
> 8 is the second term in this sequence.

tessellation
– a pattern made of identical shapes
– the shapes fit together without any gaps
– the shapes do not overlap

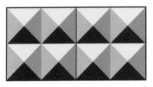

This tessellating pattern is made with triangles.

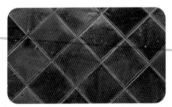

This tessellating pattern is made with squares.

tetrahedron
– a 3D shape that has four faces

thermometer
– an instrument used to measure temperature

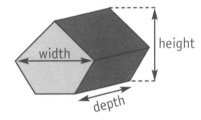

three-dimensional (3D)
– an object that has height, width and depth

width height depth

time
– the period in which things happen

It takes Tom 17 minutes to eat breakfast.

time line

– a diagram used to show the length of time between things happening

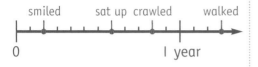

timetable

– a table where times are organised for when things happen

– examples are bus timetables, school timetables, TV timetables

Train Timetable			
Departure			Station
A	B	C	
20:43	06:58	12:53	Sydney
20:54	07:09	13:04	Strathfield
21:26	07:41	13:36	Campbelltown
22:31	08:46	14:41	Moss Vale
23:19	09:34	15:29	Goulburn

times

– another word for multiply

3 times 8 is the same as 3 × 8.

tonne

– a unit of mass

– 1000 kilograms = 1 tonne

– abbreviation is **t**

An elephant can weigh 7 tonnes.

top view

– what you see when you view an object from directly above it

the top view of a cup of coffee

total

– add all the numbers to find the total

5 + 19 + 32 + 6 + 18 = 80

80 is the total.

transformation

- moving a shape so that the shape does not change but it is in a different position
- reflect, translate or rotate can be used for a transformation

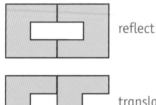 reflect

translate

rotate

translation

- moving a shape without lifting or turning it

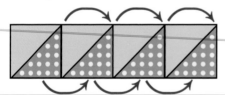

trapezium

- a special quadrilateral
- one pair of opposite sides are parallel

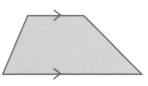

treble

- to make something three times bigger
- multiply by three

The number of strawberries has trebled.

triangle

- a polygon with three straight sides

triangular number

- a number that can make a triangular dot pattern
- one is included as a triangular number

1   3   6   10

1, 3, 6, 10 are triangular numbers.

trundle wheel

- an instrument used to measure lengths

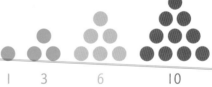

turn

– to rotate about a point

P is turning.

twelve-hour time

– time is told in 12-hour periods

– 12 midnight to 12 noon is from midnight to midday (morning) and is am time.

– 12 noon to 12 midnight is from midday to midnight (afternoon and night) and is pm time.

9 o'clock in the morning is 9 am.
9 o'clock in the evening is 9 pm.

twenty-four hour time

– time is told in 24-hour periods (1 day = 24 hours)

– 4 digits are used

9:30 am in 24-hour time is written as 0930 or 09:30.

2:45 pm in 24-hour time is written as 1445 or 14:45.

two-dimensional (2D)

– a shape that only has two dimensions; length and width (height)

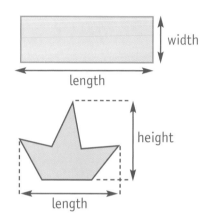

width

length

height

length

U

unequal (≠)
– not equal to

$$7 + 4 \neq 5 + 8$$

unit
– a unit is one
– units are recorded in the ONES column

Hundreds	Tens	Ones
	3	7

3 tens and 7 units

units of measurement
– standard units

Units of length include millimetre, centimetre, metre, kilometre.

Units of time include second, minute, hour, day, week, month, year, decade.

unlikely
– less than an even chance of happening but not impossible

value
- what something is worth

The value of the coin is twenty pence.

◆ + 4 = 10
The value of ◆ is 6.
The value of 7 in 2740 is 700.

variable
- a quantity which is represented by a symbol and can have different values

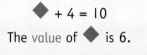 + ★ = 6

 and ★ are variables.
They can have many values,
eg = 1 and ★ = 5 or
 = 4 and ★ = 2.

Venn diagram
- shows information using circles inside a rectangle

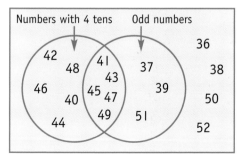

Numbers with 4 tens   Odd numbers

42 48 41 37 36
        43   38
46 40 45 47 39 50
        49 51
44   52

vertex
- the corner of a shape
- the plural of vertex is vertices

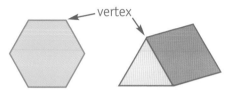

vertex

vertical
- at right angles to the horizon

The tree trunks are vertical.

volume
- the amount of space an object occupies

Volume = 2 × 2 × 2
= 8 cubic units

Units of volume:
cubic centimetres (cm^3)
cubic metres (m^3)

week
- a time period of seven days
- Sunday, Monday, Tuesday, Wednesday, Thursday, Friday, Saturday

weight
- the heaviness of an object

Sweets are often sold by weight.

whole
- all of something
- a whole number does not include a fraction or decimal

6, 94, 1053
are all whole numbers.

width
- how wide a thing is

The width of this CD is 12 cm.

12 cm

winter
- the season that follows autumn
- December, January, February

X

x

- the letter x is often used in algebra to stand for an unknown number

$$4 + x = 9$$
$$\text{so } x = 5$$

Y

year

- a time period of 12 months
- starts on 1st January and ends on 31st December
- has 365 days in a normal year and 366 days in a leap year
- Earth makes one complete revolution around the sun in one year

Each new year starts on 1st January.

Z

zero

- a place holder
- has no value
- the number between -1 and 1

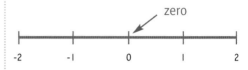

Symbols

$+$	add		π	pi ($\approx 3 \cdot 14$)
$-$	subtract		$^{\circ}$	degree
$\times$	multiply		$^{\circ}C$	degree Celsius
$\div$	divide		∞	infinity

$<$	less than		$\leftrightarrow$	line
$>$	more than		$\perp$	perpendicular to
$\leq$	less than or equal to		⌐	right angle
$\geq$	more than or equal to		⟹	parallel lines
$=$	equal to		⧧	lines of equal length
$\neq$	not equal to		$(\ )$	brackets
$\approx$	approximately equal to			

^{2}	(7^{2}) squared
^{3}	(7^{3}) cubed
$\sqrt{}$	square root
$\sqrt[3]{}$	cube root

$\%$	percent
$\bullet$	($6 \cdot 4$) decimal point

Abbreviations

mm	millimetre
cm	centimetre
m	metre
km	kilometre
mm²	square millimetre
cm²	square centimetre
m²	square metre
km²	square kilometre
ha	hectare
cm³	cubic centimetre
m³	cubic metre

g	gram
kg	kilogram
t	tonne

ml	millilitre
l	litre

am	anti meridiem (morning)
pm	post meridiem (afternoon, evening)

Equivalent fraction/decimal/percentage table

Fraction	Decimal	Percentage
$\frac{1}{2}$	0·5	50%
$\frac{1}{3}$	0·$\dot{3}$	$33\frac{1}{3}$%
$\frac{1}{4}$	0·25	25%
$\frac{3}{4}$	0·75	75%
$\frac{1}{5}$	0·2	20%
$\frac{2}{5}$	0·4	40%
$\frac{3}{5}$	0·6	60%
$\frac{4}{5}$	0·8	80%
$\frac{1}{8}$	0·125	$12\frac{1}{2}$%
$\frac{3}{8}$	0·375	$37\frac{1}{2}$%
$\frac{1}{10}$	0·1	10%
$\frac{1}{20}$	0·05	5%
$\frac{1}{100}$	0·01	1%

Roman numerals

I	= 1		VI	= 6
II	= 2		VII	= 7
III	= 3		VIII	= 8
IV	= 4		IX	= 9
V	= 5		X	= 10

X	= 10		LX	= 60
XX	= 20		LXX	= 70
XXX	= 30		LXXX	= 80
XL	= 40		XC	= 90
L	= 50		C	= 100

C	= 100		DC	= 600
CC	= 200		DCC	= 700
CCC	= 300		DCCC	= 800
CD	= 400		CM	= 900
D	= 500		M	= 1000

Measurement

Length

10 mm = 1 cm

100 cm = 1 m

1000 m = 1 km

Mass

1000 g = 1 kg

1000 kg = 1 t

Capacity

1000 ml = 1 l

Area

$100 \text{ mm}^2 = 1 \text{ cm}^2$

$10\,000 \text{ cm}^2 = 1 \text{ m}^2$

$10\,000 \text{ m}^2 = 1 \text{ ha}$

$100 \text{ ha} = 1 \text{ km}^2$

Time

60 seconds = 1 minute

60 minutes = 1 hour

24 hours = 1 day

7 days = 1 week

14 days = 2 weeks = 1 fortnight

365 days = 1 year

366 days = 1 leap year

12 months = 1 year

10 years = 1 decade

100 years = 1 century

1000 years = 1 millennium

Days in months

30 days has September,

April, June and November.

All the rest have 31

Except February alone,

Which has 28 days clear

And 29 days each leap year.

Conversion tables

Converting from Imperial measurement to Metric measurement and vice versa (correct to two decimal places)

Length

Imperial to Metric

1 inch (in)	2·54 centimetre (cm)
1 foot (ft)	30·48 cm
1 yard (yd)	0·91 metre (m)
1 mile	1·61 kilometre (km)

Metric to Imperial

1 cm	0·39 in
1 m	1·09 yd
1 km	0·62 mile

Area

Imperial to Metric

1 acre	4046·87 m²
	0·40 hectare (ha)

Metric to Imperial

1 ha	2·47 acres

Capacity

Imperial to Metric

1 fluid ounce	28·41 millilitre (ml)
1 pint (pt)	0·57 litre (l)
1 gallon (gal)	4·55 l

Metric to Imperial

1 l	1·76 pt

Mass

Imperial to Metric

1 ounce (oz)	28·35 gram (g)
1 pound (lb)	0·45 kilogram (kg)
1 stone	6·35 kg
1 ton	1·02 tonne (t)

Metric to Imperial

1 g	0·04 oz
1 kg	2·20 lb
1 t	0·98 ton

Polygons

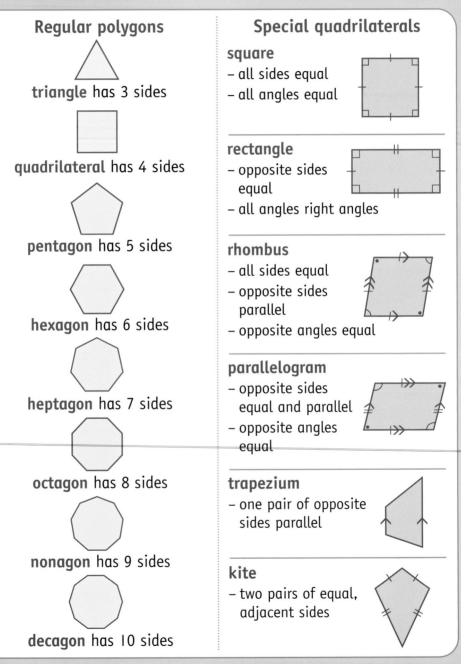

Regular polygons

triangle has 3 sides

quadrilateral has 4 sides

pentagon has 5 sides

hexagon has 6 sides

heptagon has 7 sides

octagon has 8 sides

nonagon has 9 sides

decagon has 10 sides

Special quadrilaterals

square
– all sides equal
– all angles equal

rectangle
– opposite sides
  equal
– all angles right angles

rhombus
– all sides equal
– opposite sides
  parallel
– opposite angles equal

parallelogram
– opposite sides
  equal and parallel
– opposite angles
  equal

trapezium
– one pair of opposite
  sides parallel

kite
– two pairs of equal,
  adjacent sides

Multiplication table

x	1	2	3	4	5	6	7	8	9	10
1	1	2	3	4	5	6	7	8	9	10
2	2	4	6	8	10	12	14	16	18	20
3	3	6	9	12	15	18	21	24	27	30
4	4	8	12	16	20	24	28	32	36	40
5	5	10	15	20	25	30	35	40	45	50
6	6	12	18	24	30	36	42	48	54	60
7	7	14	21	28	35	42	49	56	63	70
8	8	16	24	32	40	48	56	64	72	80
9	9	18	27	36	45	54	63	72	81	90
10	10	20	30	40	50	60	70	80	90	100

Angles

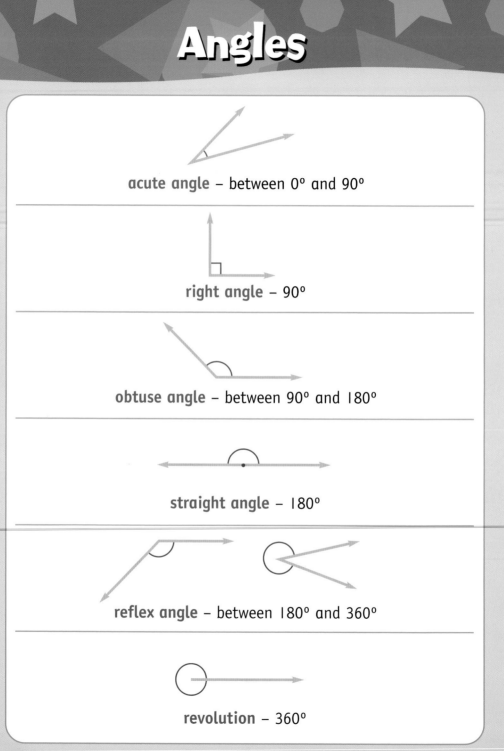

acute angle – between 0º and 90º

right angle – 90º

obtuse angle – between 90º and 180º

straight angle – 180º

reflex angle – between 180º and 360º

revolution – 360º

Triangles

Scalene triangle
- all sides are different lengths
- all angles are different sizes

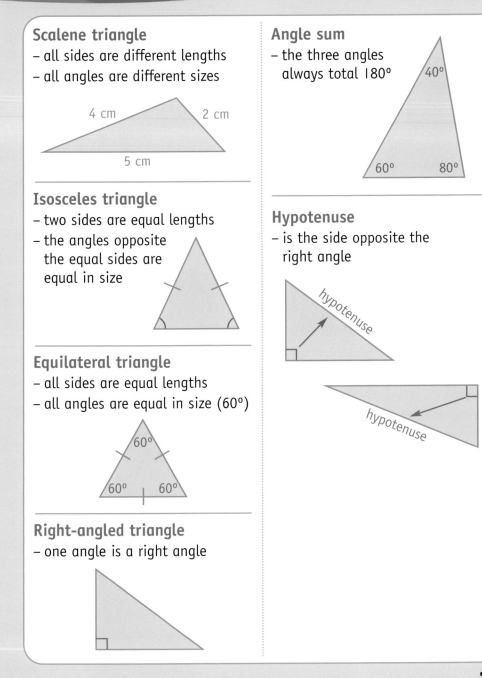

Isosceles triangle
- two sides are equal lengths
- the angles opposite the equal sides are equal in size

Equilateral triangle
- all sides are equal lengths
- all angles are equal in size (60°)

Right-angled triangle
- one angle is a right angle

Angle sum
- the three angles always total 180°

Hypotenuse
- is the side opposite the right angle

3D objects

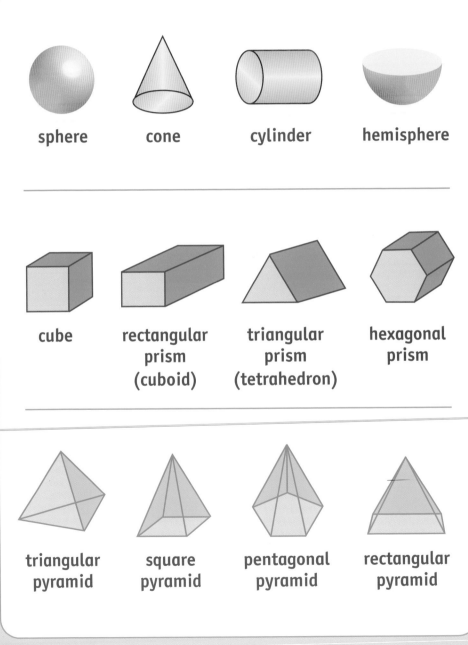

sphere

cone

cylinder

hemisphere

cube

rectangular prism (cuboid)

triangular prism (tetrahedron)

hexagonal prism

triangular pyramid

square pyramid

pentagonal pyramid

rectangular pyramid

Squared and cubed numbers

Squares

$1^2 = 1$

$2^2 = 4$

$3^2 = 9$

$4^2 = 16$

$5^2 = 25$

$6^2 = 36$

$7^2 = 49$

$8^2 = 64$

$9^2 = 81$

$10^2 = 100$

Square roots

$\sqrt{1} = 1$

$\sqrt{4} = 2$

$\sqrt{9} = 3$

$\sqrt{16} = 4$

$\sqrt{25} = 5$

$\sqrt{36} = 6$

$\sqrt{49} = 7$

$\sqrt{64} = 8$

$\sqrt{81} = 9$

$\sqrt{100} = 10$

Cubes

$1^3 = 1$

$2^3 = 8$

$3^3 = 27$

$4^3 = 64$

$5^3 = 125$

$6^3 = 216$

$7^3 = 343$

$8^3 = 512$

$9^3 = 729$

$10^3 = 1000$

Cube roots

$\sqrt[3]{1} = 1$

$\sqrt[3]{8} = 2$

$\sqrt[3]{27} = 3$

$\sqrt[3]{64} = 4$

$\sqrt[3]{125} = 5$

$\sqrt[3]{216} = 6$

$\sqrt[3]{343} = 7$

$\sqrt[3]{512} = 8$

$\sqrt[3]{729} = 9$

$\sqrt[3]{1000} = 10$

Prime numbers to 100

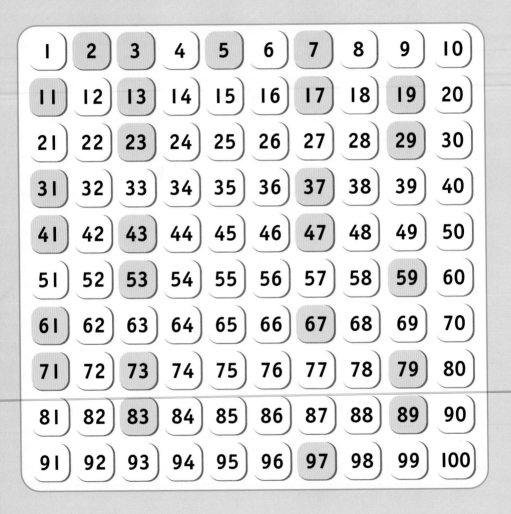